THE FRIDAY

MORNING CLUB

A FABLE OF CHANCE, WEALTH, AND LEGACY

FRANK REILLY

ISBN 978-1-936961-41-2

Books are available for special promotions and premiums.

For details, contact:

Special Markets
LINX
Box 613
Great Falls, VA 22066

E-mail: specialmarkets@linxcorp.com

Published by LINX

DEDICATION

To my loving wife, who has always journeyed with me no matter where we go. Whether it is moving halfway around the world, safaris on the African savannah, or working with elephants in the jungles of Thailand. Nothing would have been possible without you.

And to all of our clients. We are humbled by the immense trust you place in us with your hard-earned wealth, and we are dedicated to working hard every day to continue earning that trust.

ACKNOWLEDGEMENTS

To all of the Reilly Financial Advisors employees who make it a joy to come to work each day.

TABLE OF CONTENTS

PART 1:
THE AWAKENING

ERIC

The fifty-two-year-old founder of FinSoft Engineering never planned on being a wildly successful Silicon Valley CEO. But success smiled on this son of a retired GM factory worker from Ohio, who had a knack for developing hugely popular software programs and apps that were worth millions.

His first big success was the program he created to help small vendors conduct secure online transactions. After the program became a huge hit, one of the Valley's big tech companies bought it for over $6 million, leading Eric to relocate his company from Dayton to Palo Alto.

The hits kept on coming. During its first year in the Valley, FinSoft developed a popular new program that helped consumers manage online coupons and other discounts, and an app that compiled and analyzed consumers' social media data for national retail chains.

"SUCCESS"

Eric was grateful for FinSoft's rapid growth, but success had also brought stress.

Always more of an engineer than an entrepreneur, Eric never planned on being a corporate CEO. He knew his biggest strength was his technical expertise in solving complex problems, not executive leadership. But once he realized nobody else cared more about FinSoft's future success than he did, he sought out experts and mentors—like his good friend Bill—to help him handle the many personnel and economic challenges his company faced.

The company struggled during the Great Recession, but over the last five years FinSoft had grown wildly profitable. Even after rewarding top employees with generous bonuses, Eric still did pretty well himself, taking home $1 million to $2 million in earnings in each of the last five years.

But his sudden wealth aroused complicated and conflicting feelings. While thankful for his success, he also felt uncomfortable. His father, Gene, had always griped at the dinner table about "fat cats" and "financiers," implying that people who had a lot of money had probably also:

a. Done immoral and unethical things to acquire their wealth;

b. Used their money and power to keep little guys like Gene under their thumbs in a state of perpetual serfdom.

The way Eric saw things now, money wasn't good or bad. Money's neutral. It's *people* who made good or bad decisions about whatever money they had.

As long as FinSoft's bottom trended ever upward, Eric remained focused on creating the company's next big hit. He was glad to be part of the Valley's millionaire's club, and grateful that his success had opened the door for him to meet two people who had enriched and changed his life, especially his wife, Hitomi.

LOVE AND FAMILY

As a teenager, Hitomi had won a contest for Japanese students studying robotics. After graduating from high school, she migrated to America so she could study at Stanford University's robotics and artificial intelligence lab, where she majored in learning and motion, graduating with an M.A. and honors.

Hitomi went to work for one of the Valley's big AI start-ups, rising through the ranks to become a leading researcher, but she was equally committed to starting a family. While she had met hundreds of eligible men in the Valley, there was something different about Eric. He seemed more balanced and humble than the many Valley visionaries who were convinced they were single-handedly changing the world for the better.

Their relationship progressed the way things in the Valley often do: at warp speed. Family was paramount for Hitomi, who balanced work and family duties by reducing her workload to raise their girls before returning to full-time work when they started school.

A little over a quarter century later, Eric and Hitomi celebrated the success of their two daughters. Twenty-five-year-old Emma recently married her sweetheart, Heinrich, a regional director for an international charity. Twenty-two-year-old Isabella just finished her bachelor's degree in aerospace engineering and next will pursue a graduate degree in astronomy so she can work in the space industry.

Eric was happy about his family. They gave him a deep joy he didn't experience at work. And he was glad he could provide things for them that his father had never been able to afford: great schools and lessons for the kids, travel, charitable giving, and a succession of ever-larger homes.

GROWING PAINS

Eric operated his business on the basis of two simple slogans that had, over time, become sort of an unofficial company motto:

- *Move Forward!* Don't look back over your shoulder at the solutions or successes of the past. Look forward to the opportunities of tomorrow.

- *Move Faster!* Time is of the essence. Many companies are working to solve the same problems, but the company that finds the best solution first will be victorious.

Overall, these minimalist maxims served their purpose, helping make FinSoft lean, mean, and rapid to respond to new technological challenges.

But FinSoft's continuing growth added to Eric's workload and stress.

"I already feel like I'm running as fast as I possibly can," he told his friend and mentor, Bill. "But each new challenge means I need to run even faster."

FinSoft added more junior executives and dozens of programmers so it could expand into new business ventures, adding to the pressures that weighed on Eric. But Eric still wasn't ready to bring on a Chief Operating Officer (COO) to help him manage the company, as some of his advisors suggested.

Eric wished he could call a "Time Out" in his life and career so he could sort out his thoughts and plot a good path forward. That's why he was so happy when Bill called and invited him to Baja, Mexico.

BILL

Over his long life, Bill had worn many hats: inventor, entrepreneur, airplane pilot and amateur mechanic, and world explorer. Over the last decade, Bill has gone from being someone Eric would run into occasionally at high-tech gatherings in the Valley to becoming one of Eric's dearest and most trusted friends.

Bill's family were Silicon Valley pioneers. His grandfather joined Hewlett-Packard in the early 1940s, cashing in on the company's explosive growth and generating the family's initial wealth, which had grown phenomenally ever since.

Bill was a handsome, muscular grandfather who looked much younger than his sixty-six years. He said part of what kept him young was coaching younger executives like Eric.

Their friendship developed in stages. Bill was one of the first "Valley old-timers" Eric met after relocating his company from Ohio. They would often sit together at community business lunches and meetings, comparing notes on new "world-changing" technologies, and sharing an occasional laugh when hot-shot entrepreneurs displayed reason-defying confidence in their plans for global domination.

Most of all, Eric noticed how Bill—unlike so many other locals—seemed to have time to listen to Eric and engage him in long, thoughtful conversations.

Over time the two grew closer, meeting for occasional breakfasts, lunches, or dinners, when Eric could pour out his concerns and Bill would gently talk him down off the ledge. Eric trusted Bill. He always felt better about things after these meetings, and he frequently used Bill's advice when confronting difficult decisions.

As soon as Eric and Hitomi had Bill over for dinner at their home, she could immediately see why her husband had developed such a deep friendship with this wise, open-hearted man.

Over time, Bill could see that Eric was suffering from a common ailment he called "Valley Fever."

"You have all these guys who are doing their darndest to revolutionize major industries in the next week or two," said Bill, describing the ailment he had seen too many times. "But after a while, they just become too worn out and worn down. They become empty shells of their former selves."

Seeing Eric exhibiting increasing symptoms of Valley Fever, Bill invited him to accompany him on one of his favorite adventures: his annual February flight to Baja, Mexico to see the calving and migration of gray whales.

DATE WITH DESTINY

Eric felt a wave of relief wash over him the moment Bill's plane lifted off from the San Jose airport. Within a few hours they would be visiting the lagoons hidden away on the southernmost tip of Baja. At times they watched the whales from a distance, and at other times it felt they could nearly touch these majestic creatures from the small skiff Bill rented from a local fisherman.

For the next four days, the two men followed the whales, ate relaxed meals, drank too many beers, had detailed discussions about Eric's biggest business concerns, and waded into deep philosophical discussions about work-life balance and the meaning of it all.

Then, just as Eric was feeling deeply relaxed, it was time to head back home. Eric had enjoyed the break with Bill so much that he somewhat dreaded returning to his life in the Valley.

They were a little more than halfway home when one of the engines started making a funny sound.

"It's just a little carburetor cough," said Bill, smiling and fiddling with a gas line. "Everything will be fine in a minute."

Ten minutes later, the engine continued to gurgle and the plane continued to lose altitude.

Bill now looked worried. It was the first time Eric had ever seen him panicked, and he didn't like the sight.

As Eric pictured himself falling to his death in this remote section of the ocean off the coast of Mexico, his anxieties rose to the surface. Three main questions wracked his mind:

What would Hitomi do? She's a strong woman, but how would she handle the turmoil his death would bring to FinSoft? And could she manage the family's growing wealth?

Who will take care of my beautiful girls? Eric talked to his two daughters every week, sometimes almost every day. Who would watch out for them now?

Who is going to run FinSoft? Eric had failed to end a destructive power struggle among some of his junior executives. Right now, he had no idea which of the young men and women currently jockeying for supremacy would wind up controlling the company's future.

A FRIDAY FRIENDSHIP

After another few tense moments of fiddling and fixing, Bill was finally able to bring the engine back to life. Neither man spoke for a while as the plane gradually regained speed and altitude.

In time, they could see familiar Valley landmarks. That's when Eric made his proposal.

"Bill, I really want to thank you for this trip and the things it has made me think about."

"It was my pleasure," said Bill. "And I'm glad we both have a bit more time to remember it!"

"Me too," said Eric. "And to celebrate, I have an idea."

Eric asked Bill if the two of them could meet weekly to discuss the many business and family issues that were making Eric anxious.

"Of course," said Bill. "And since today's a Friday, let's meet on Fridays for breakfast or lunch."

And that's how the two-member "Friday Morning Club" got its start.

PART 2:
FINDING THE BALANCE

LIFE, DEATH, AND OMELETS

It took them a while to synchronize their schedules, but Bill and Eric finally met for breakfast early on a Friday morning three weeks after their near-fatal ride in Bill's plane. They met at Bill's Café, a popular but unassuming breakfast spot in South San Jose.

"Don't worry," Bill told Eric as the two men sat down in a booth. "I've got no relationship to the Bill who owns the restaurant, so I'm not making any profit on our meal!"

They ordered and quickly caught up.

"So, how have things been going?" Bill asked.

Eric was slow in responding.

"It's complicated, but one thing's for sure. I've never been so glad to be alive, and part of that is because I've never come so close before to *not* being alive!"

"Yeah," said Bill. "There's nothing like a close brush with death to make you rethink life."

Bill's comment wasn't theoretical, but was based on lengthy personal experience. During the two years he had served in the Air Force in the final years of the Vietnam War, he quickly gave up keeping track of his many fellow pilots who lost their lives to enemy antiaircraft artillery.

"I saw dozens of men fly off and never return," said Bill, "but somehow I always came back in one piece."

Eric's near-fatal flight with Bill was his first real brush with death, and memories of the experience disturbed him during the coming weeks. He told Bill he'd had two panic attacks and a handful of sleepless nights.

"I never really realized how suddenly things can turn around," said Eric. "It's shocking that one minute you feel like you are on top of the world, and then POOF, the next minute you could just totally disappear."

"You should be grateful," said Bill. "Many people don't wake up to their own mortality until they're lying on their deathbed. But you've been given an early preview. This is a wake-up call, a chance to live your life in a new way. Don't blow it."

"I hear you, but that doesn't mean I know what my next steps should be."

"Well," said Bill, "let's talk about that a bit more over breakfast next week."

"Sounds great," said Eric.

"Meanwhile, remember to take a deep breath now and then. And give Hitomi an extra hug."

"Believe me, I'm already doing that."

WORK, AND EVERYTHING ELSE

Meeting at Bill's Café for breakfast a week later, Bill tried to focus in on Eric's workaholism and growing stress. He also wanted to circle back to an earlier discussion the two men had had when Eric expressed his ambivalence about bringing on a Chief Operating Officer to help him manage his growing company.

"There's this thing people talk about called work-life balance," Bill said. "Have you ever heard of that? What do you think of the current balance in your own life?"

"Balance?" joked Eric. "What's that?"

Growing up, Eric had heard frequent sermons on the religion of work from his father, Gene, who spent three decades working at a GM factory outside Dayton, Ohio.

"It's work that makes a man," Gene would say, pounding the dinner table, "and it's how a man works that shows you what he is made of."

Eric took these sermons to heart and did his best to follow his father's example by working as hard as he could. Instead of pursuing sports or other activities in school, he worked numerous newspaper delivery routes. He spent his summers mowing neighbors' lawns and his winters shoveling their driveways.

He worked his way through college, and once he founded FinSoft Engineering shortly after graduation, he pushed himself even harder.

"I am working for myself now," Eric had said, "so working harder makes more sense."

FinSoft's success had caught Eric by surprise, and once he made his few first million and relocated to Silicon Valley, the only thing he knew to do was to push himself even harder and work longer hours, even though he knew his lifestyle was bad for his health and his marriage.

"A few months ago, you told me you felt like you were running as fast as you could," Bill said. "Is that still the case?"

"Yes," Eric admitted. "It's actually worse than before."

"What you think about that?"

"I'm getting tired of it," Eric said. "That's not the way I want to live my life. Whether I die a week from now or thirty years from now, I want there to be something else in my life other than work."

"So, what do you think of finally acting on your earlier idea to bring on a COO? Do you think that can help you?"

"I think it could," Eric said, "but I'm just not sure I'm ready for that."

"What would make you ready? What could make you actually hire a COO instead of continuing to think about it as you continue to gripe about how much you work?"

Eric felt like he was in a jam, and there was no way out.

"I guess the thing I worry about most is getting the wrong person, which would make everything worse."

"But there's another possibility," said Bill. "You could hire the right person. How would that look?"

"Awesome," said Eric. "I can't tell you what a relief that would be."

"Well, how about this. Next Friday you and I can talk about what kind of person would make the perfect COO. And then, if you like, I can introduce you to some of my headhunter friends. These are personnel experts who may have your ideal candidate on their Rolodex."

"It would be great if you could walk me through this," Eric said.

"OK," said Bill. "I would be glad to be your tour guide!"

"SO, WHAT ARE YOU AFRAID OF?"

Bill and Eric spent the next two Fridays hammering out their description of the perfect COO for Eric's company. Overall, Eric was ready to change how things ran at FinSoft, particularly when he contemplated what it would be like to finally have a life outside of work. But there still remained areas that Eric was fearful of turning over.

"Well, what are you actually afraid of?" Bill asked.

"Basically, everything," said Eric. "I'm fine trusting someone else to help me share the burden of leading the company, but I'm scared of what could happen if I'm left out of the loop on important decisions."

"I think you can make sure that doesn't happen," said Bill. "So, are you ready to do this?"

"I wasn't ready before, but I am now," said Eric.

"Okay. It's time to contact one of the experts."

Bill reviewed with Eric the pros and cons of some of the main headhunting firms in the Valley, recommending the one firm he believed would be best to handle Eric's situation.

"These guys have done this hundreds of times with companies bigger than yours," he said. "They can help you if you let them do it."

"Okay," said Eric. "Will you handle the phone introduction?"

"I'm glad to," said Bill.

Within a couple of weeks, the firm found three solid candidates. Six weeks later, Eric and his board picked the company's new COO.

A VALUE BEYOND MEASURE

It had been a busy few weeks, but when Bill and Eric caught up for breakfast again, Eric was excited.

"Thank you, thank you, thank you," said Eric. "I offer you a million thanks for helping me get some of my life back."

"What do you mean?"

"Your headhunter friends certainly know what they're doing. We found a great candidate, and even though this transition period will take some work, I've already decided to take a week off after our new COO settles in.

"Plus, Hitomi and I have already been looking at interesting places where we can go. It will be the first time we've had a week off together in years. I can't wait, and she seems even happier about it than I am."

A big smile broke out on Eric's face. This was the clearest demonstration of joy Bill had seen in his friend during all the months they been talking and all the years they had seen each other at various Valley industry events.

"So, what is it that makes you feel so darned happy about this?"

"I guess over the years I just forgot how big a deal it is to have fun once in a while."

"How big a deal is it?"

Eric looked at his omelet for a moment.

"There's no way to put a dollar value on it," said Eric. "I guess you could say it's priceless."

"Some of the best things in life are," said Bill. "Real wealth can't be measured in money."

"I guess I've always known that deep down, but somehow it escaped me while I had my attention laser-focused on everything else."

Bill grew philosophical.

"People are easily confused," he said. "Some of the wealthiest people I know in this Valley lead miserable lives. They've got everything, but they enjoy nothing. Meanwhile, some of the people who have the least in terms of finances seem to have the most in terms of relational wealth."

Bill told Eric about a recent mission trip his church took to Guatemala.

"We go down there every year to help groups by painting their buildings, or even building new structures or water wells.

But while we're busy trying to help them, these people come alongside us and help us. They are some of the most joyful and alive people I have ever seen, and they do it all on a few dollars a day. Simply amazing."

Eric had never planned on amassing great financial wealth. He just knew he needed to work, and he worked hard until the money came. Now he was feeling adrift.

"It seems like somewhere along the way I just lost track of some of the things that really mattered."

"Look at your life," said Bill. "You possess many things in abundance that other people would die for. You have your health. You have a roof over your head, food to eat, and clothes to wear. You have meaningful work. You have a wife who loves you and two beautiful daughters who are making their way in the world. Then, on top of all that, you have more money than most people could spend in a lifetime. Do you ever stop and think about the value of all these wonderful gifts?"

"Not really," said Eric.

"You gave me a million thanks this morning. Try saying some thanks once in a while for all these great gifts you have been given."

"I think I'll give that a try," Eric said.

A CALL FOR HELP

Daughter Emma met Heinrich while pursuing her degree in international law and finance. Now the two of them were working together with RefugeeAssist, an international charity working to help some of the world's 68 million refugees.

Mother and daughter still tried to have their weekly phone call, even though Emma's work in Pakistan sometimes made that difficult. And in her latest call, Emma told Hitomi about a campaign the charity was organizing to help the record-high number of refugees in the world.

"We are asking governments, businesses, and individuals to make significant donations to help people fleeing war, genocide, and famine. And I thought, why don't I put my money where my mouth is by making a significant donation myself?"

Emma explained that she would like to take some of her "future inheritance" now so she could contribute to the refugee campaign.

"I really want to help these people," Emma said.

After Hitomi told Eric about the call with Emma, Eric took a moment before responding.

"I respect what Emma's saying, but there's just one problem," Eric said. "Emma doesn't have an inheritance set up for her yet. That has been on my to-do list for years, but it never got to the top the list."

Frankly, their family finances were poorly organized, but as long as the cash kept flowing in, Eric had never made it a priority to prepare for his or his family's future.

Eric and Bill met for breakfast two days later, and Eric talked to Bill about Emma requesting part of her "future inheritance."

"The whole thing makes me feel like I've failed to take care of things like I should have," Eric said.

"Well," said Bill, "there are a few things you could've done to better prepare for the future, but you still have time to prepare if you want to.

"And take it from me, you're not the only person who came to this town to follow a dream, and who became wealthy following that dream, but who didn't have a clue about what they wanted to do with their wealth. You should see some of the con jobs and questionable investments I've seen people fall for."

"The thing is," Eric said, "I grew up never having much money, so I never really learned how to take care of it. Plus, my dad always assumed that 'fat cats' probably acquired their wealth by questionable means. And now that I'm a fat cat, I guess I'm not sure how to deal with that."

Bill was smiling.

"You know, the funny thing is, I know plenty of fat cats out here who would be excited to have a daughter who wanted to give some money to a charity," Bill said. "These guys are worried about sons and daughters blowing their inheritance on tricked-out cars, or gambling debts from too many weekends in Vegas, or drugs. You should be happy."

Before, Eric had thought he was the only one. Now he realized other tech titans wrestled with the same issues.

"That part of it actually did make me happy. I'm so glad Emma has a big heart for the world. But her request made me realize that I've dropped the ball."

"Well," Bill said. "They say that failing to plan is planning to fail. And frankly, most of the time out here it seems like more people are planning to fail than are planning to succeed.

"But you still have time, and if you use the time wisely, you can avoid the horror story guys out here in the Valley talk about. They call it 'from shirtsleeves to shirtsleeves in three generations.'"

"What the heck is that?" Eric asked.

"Well, it goes like this. Generation one is somebody like you, a shirtsleeves person who works hard, comes up with a good idea, packages and sells that idea, and reaps the rewards.

"Generation two is that couple's sons and daughters. They don't realize the work and sweat and hardship that went into dad's and mom's success. All they know is that the family is swimming in money, and they dive in.

"Generation three is the children of these sons and daughters. Most of the wealth their grandparents generated was frittered away by their parents, and now generation three is back to working in their shirtsleeves, trying to make it, trying to come up with the next big thing."

Bill described a few of the horror stories he had seen as members of generation two busily burned through money like it was never going to dry up.

"Some of these shirtsleeve founders would love to see one of their kids doing something charitable with their money," Bill said. "At least that leaves a positive mark on the world."

Eric was taking it all in.

"So, what kind of conversations have you had with your kids about money?"

"We've never done that," said Eric. "The company really began going gangbusters right at the same time we were raising the girls. Everything just happened all together, and we never really sat down and sorted it all out."

"Are you ready to start sorting it out now?" Bill asked.

"Let's talk about that in a couple weeks after I get back to town."

THE GETAWAY

Eric and Hitomi had a short list of goals they considered essential for their upcoming getaway vacation.

Quiet. It seemed daily life was getting noisier by the day, so they yearned for a bit of solitude and silence.

Remote. They wanted to go somewhere they had never been before (and somewhere they wouldn't run into anyone connected to their hectic lives in the Valley).

Beauty. Both seemed to believe that experiencing the grandeur of nature would recharge their internal batteries.

They achieved all three goals with their decision to attend Newfoundland's annual iceberg festival, celebrated every June on the northwesternmost tip of Newfoundland. This wild, magical place where the Gulf of St. Lawrence meets the Labrador Sea was also the spot where Vikings had first settled in North America a thousand years ago.

Everything was more quiet, remote, and beautiful than they could have hoped. When they weren't busy marveling at the sights and history of the place, they were busy talking to each other like they hadn't talked in years.

Hitomi had been more intensely focused on Eric in the months since his near-death experience with Bill near Baja, Mexico. She hectored him into visiting a doctor and a dentist, people he hadn't seen in years.

"I need you to take better care of yourself," she pleaded with him.

Finally alone together for what seemed like the first time in years, they easily fell into deep conversations that reminded them of the all-night talks they enjoyed when they fell in love with each other more than a quarter-century earlier.

They spent their last evening in Newfoundland at a restaurant having dinner, drinking wine, and watching icebergs bob in the churning waters. Over the course of three-and-a-half hours, they delved into a series of three important questions:

1. *What kind of life do we want for ourselves in the coming years?*

2. *What kind of lives do we want for our daughters and their families?*

3. *And what about FinSoft?*

   They rarely talked about the details of the company, and

that meant Hitomi often felt "left out." She didn't want it to be that way anymore.

"I want to be more involved in helping you make some of the hard decisions that I see weighing you down."

4. *And aside from our family and the company, what kind of impact or legacy do we want to leave on the world, today and after we are gone?*

It was a great way to end a wonderful week away, but then the next morning, it was off to the airport for a return to normal life. And once they were back in the Valley, everything was go-go-go. There was no time for slow meals or long talks.

As he returned to the chaos of his FinSoft office after his first real getaway in years, Eric wasn't sure he liked the fact that the place survived just fine without him for a week.

ICEBERGS

Eric was grateful for the great week away and the many good conversations with Hitomi. But once he got back into his normal Valley routine, he pretty much forgot about the whole getaway until he and Bill sat down for their next Friday morning meeting at their regular hangout, Bill's Café.

After they ordered, Eric shared photos of the giant icebergs and the historic Viking settlement.

"And we had some great conversations," Eric said, as he told Bill about the big issues he and Hitomi had discussed.

"We covered everything. But it seems like we didn't really land on anything. I guess we've never really sat back and thought about our big goals for the future, and at times it seems like our goals don't even line up."

"They're all icebergs," Bill said.

"What's all icebergs?" asked Eric, who was still on his first cup of coffee.

"All those big talks the two of you had about your future, your kids' futures, the futures of your business. They are all icebergs. What I mean is, you think you're talking about a subject that's somewhat cut and dried. But underneath the surface is a whole bunch of stuff that nobody is talking about."

"What you mean?" Eric asked.

"You said your dad preached a religion of work. Well, I would say you've been a pretty faithful follower of that religion. But now, when you try to talk with Hitomi about the kind of future the two of you want to share together, everything your father told you is part of your iceberg.

"It's all part of who you are, but it's under the surface. That's why it's an iceberg. And the thing is, you may not be aware it's even there until it bobs up to the surface during one of these deep conversations you're having.

"I'm sure Hitomi has her own icebergs. Everyone does. I've got my own icebergs that come from the way I was raised, or from seeing my fellow airmen die. Another part of my iceberg: I've been stabbed in the back a few times. Not everyone in the Valley plays fair."

"I've never thought of it that way," said Eric, "but I sure can picture how much is under the surface after my week in Newfoundland."

"There's always more under the surface that we don't see," said Bill. "Let's talk about some of that next time."

"Sounds great!"

PART 3
GOING UNDER THE SURFACE

EXPLORING ICEBERGS

"Well, look what the cat dragged in!"

That's how Bill greeted Eric when the two of them got together for their next Friday breakfast at Bill's Café.

"Good morning," said Eric, with minimal enthusiasm. His eyes were bloodshot, and his hair, which was always somewhat unruly, was wilder than usual.

"Are you okay? You look like crap," said Bill.

"I feel like crap," Eric told him. "I didn't get much sleep last night. Again."

After the two friends ordered breakfast and caught up, Eric explained his angst.

"There's this dream I have every once in a while. You and I are on our trip to Baja, and we are ready to head back home. On the way back home, your plane has engine problems.

"You can't get the engine to work again, and the plane just continues to go down, down, down for what seems like an hour.

"The whole time, I'm freaking out and asking myself all the questions that went through my mind when your engine was stalled. All I could think about was Hitomi, the girls, and the company.

"The plane keeps going down, and the ocean is getting closer, but all I can think about is who will take care of Hitomi, who will watch out for Emma and Isabella, and who will direct the future of FinSoft.

"Then, just when the plane is about to crash into the water, I wake up, panting and sweating."

"Wow," said Bill. "That doesn't sound like fun."

"No. It doesn't happen very often, but when it does, it really kind of jolts me awake, and I can't sleep anymore."

Bill looked Eric in his bloodshot eyes.

"Do you remember what we talked about last time?"

"Not really," said Eric.

"Icebergs," said Bill. "We talked about how there's always more under the surface that we don't see."

"Yeah, I remember. We talked about the icebergs I saw in Newfoundland. Then we talked about icebergs as metaphors for things in our lives that are not exposed."

"I think some of your icebergs may be causing these bad dreams of yours."

"I think you may be right."

"So, let me ask you a question."

"Shoot," said Eric.

"Have you done anything to address your concerns about Hitomi, the girls, and your company since we got back from our trip?"

Eric was slow in responding.

"I guess I haven't, not really," said Eric.

"Voilá," said Bill. "You were already worried about these three things before we went on our trip, and our near-accident only made them more dramatic. I think your dreams are your mind's way of reminding you to take care of some unfinished business."

"I think you may be right."

It was time for Eric to go to his office. As they got up to leave, Bill offered an invitation.

"How about if you and I start talking about some of these icebergs next week, assuming you can get some sleep?"

"That would be good," said Eric.

"REAL WEALTH"

"So," asked Bill, when he and Eric got together for breakfast two weeks later. "Ready to explore some icebergs?"

"Sure," said Eric. "Will I need gloves and boots?"

"No, just your mind and heart."

Bill had jotted down a series of questions he wanted to discuss with Eric in the coming weeks, starting with questions about wealth.

"So, do you think of yourself as wealthy?" he asked.

Eric paused before responding.

"I guess so, but maybe not as much as other people."

"Well, if you're comparing yourself to some of the other people here in the Valley, all of us look like we're poverty-stricken. But forget about other people for a minute. Do you think you are wealthy? Do you feel wealthy?"

"If wealthy means having more money than I may ever need, then I guess I am wealthy."

"So, is that's what wealthy means? Having more money than you need?"

"I'm not sure," Eric said. "All I know is I spent my first twenty years of life worrying about having enough money, and I spent the last five worrying about having too much money, and wondering what to do with it all. At times I think I've become one of those fat cats my dad warned me about."

"But weren't the fat cats your dad railed against unethical people who exploited others? You don't do that kind of behavior, do you?"

"I try not to do those things," said Eric. "I don't want to be that kind of rich person."

"Well, what average person do you want to be then?"

"I don't really know," Eric confessed.

"Let's talk about how wealthy you actually are by looking at the various kinds of wealth people acquire."

Bill asked Eric about the various kinds of assets he owned: cash, stocks, bonds, ownership interests, real property, etc. Eric had considerable assets, but didn't seem to be sure what all his holdings really were.

"Well, based upon that brief survey, I think I can officially declare you wealthy, at least in the financial sense! Now let's look at some other forms of wealth to see if you have those."

"What do you mean?" asked Eric.

"Well, for one thing, you have your health. That's wealth of a kind, isn't it?"

"I guess it is," said Eric. "I don't really think about health as something I possess, but I guess I do, and that's very important to me."

"Great, then. We will declare you wealthy when it comes to your health. What about your family?"

"My family is more precious to me than anything in this world."

"Well, you have a good family, a loving family. I know people in this town who would pay a lot for that. What about your name and reputation? From everything I hear, people in the Valley respect you. Is that wealth?"

"My dad always told me that a person's family name and character are the two most valuable things in life. So if you say I have a good name in the Valley, that means a lot to me personally. Plus, it is also not bad for business, is it?"

"Not bad at all. And I think there are some other assets you possess, assets that have helped make your company successful. These are your knowledge and expertise assets. You know your field, and you try to see what's coming down the pike. These are assets too, aren't they?"

"Definitely," said Eric.

"Final question," said Bill. "If you had died in the ocean off of Baja, how much of all these various kinds of wealth would have gone down with you, and what kinds of wealth would hang around?"

"I guess I'd never thought of it that way," said Eric. "Let me think. I guess my health would be gone, or irrelevant at that point. But if I actually have the kind of reputation around here that you say I have, I guess my reputation would live on, at least until people forgot all about me!"

"What about your family?"

"Well, my family would still exist, but they would be without me. And that's probably one of my major icebergs. If I had died down in Baja, I think my family would be okay, but I think they could be better off if I actually had some kind of formal plan in place to deal with all this wealth you say I have!"

"I agree," that Bill. "They probably would be, but there's much more you could do to prepare for the possibility than you've done so far."

"That's probably the case," Eric admitted.

"Okay, then. Let's take a closer look at this iceberg next time."

BRICKS

The next time Bill and Eric met, Bill had a surprise: a physical prop he wanted to use for today's discussion. He reached into his fat leather briefcase, pulled out a brick, and set it on the table.

"Deborah and I are having a walkway installed, and I thought this would make an excellent object lesson."

"Go for it," said Eric.

"Well, for the trick to work, you will need to pretend that this red brick sitting here is actually a gold brick worth millions of dollars."

"OK, I will play along."

"One thing I see happening time and time again in the Valley is that people like you spend most of their time and energy making bricks. Of course, these people are actually working to create products and services that people buy. But when people buy these products and services, that creates wealth. So, think of the gold bricks as repositories of that wealth."

"OK," said Eric. "Makes sense."

"Then, life happens. In some cases, the brick makers get older, and they realize they have more bricks than they will ever need. So, they start thinking about how they're going to pass on the bricks to their loved ones. Or, they die in a plane crash off Baja, and suddenly the other family members need to figure out how they can manage all these gold bricks.

"But much of the time, what I see people like you doing is basically throwing bricks. The picture I see is the business owner standing on one side of a wall, hurling bricks over the wall to his family members on the opposite side. There's no real communication between the parties, just bricks flying over a wall.

"Sometimes, family members are ready and are expecting these bricks to come flying over the fence, so they catch the bricks, using them for expenses or saving them for later.

"But much of the time, the people on the other side of the wall aren't prepared, and they're surprised when these bricks start flying over the wall.

"And in some cases, these heavy, flying bricks actually hit the people they are intended to help, hurting them, and messing up their lives. That tension is what happened in the John Grisham novel, *The Testament*. There's a billionaire who's getting old, and he needs to do something about his bricks. Meanwhile, family members are circling like vultures. The billionaire knows that some family members would only use the bricks to subsidize their lazy, lecherous lifestyles.

"You've probably seen cases here in the Valley with business owners who try to pass on great sums of wealth to members of the next generation, but in the process they sometimes wind up hurting the very people they are trying to help."

"I've seen this happen more times than I care to remember," Eric said.

"Bingo," said Bill. "That's my point. I'm trying to avoid that with you and your bricks. I don't want you throwing bricks at Hitomi and the girls. I want the three of you to be on the same page about what's happening with all these bricks."

Eric looked down at his hash browns.

"Well, maybe you ought to just hit me with a brick!"

"What do you mean?" Bill asked.

"Ever since I started to make real money out here, I've been planning to sit down and talk to the family about our bricks. But that conversation never seems to happen. And if it did happen, I'm not even sure I would know what to say."

"Double bingo," said Bill. "We've got our topic for our next breakfast. Hopefully we can come up with a better plan than just throwing bricks over a wall."

"I hope so too!" said Eric.

THE CONVERSATION

"You will be proud of me," Eric told Bill when the two met for breakfast the following week. "I did some extra-credit reading!"

"Excellent," said Bill. "What was the topic?"

"Having the talk with your kids," Eric said. "Not the talk about the birds and the bees, but the money talk."

"Oh," said Bill. "Nice. Both talks are important, and both can make parents nervous. So, what did you think about what you read?"

"There was an article in *The Wall Street Journal* about how and when to talk to your kids about money. We've never really talked to our girls about money very much, other than to let them know that they will never go hungry or to be homeless. Besides that, we haven't talked much at all about it."

"That's why it remains an iceberg," said Bill. "There's still so much under the surface that you and the kids haven't explored."

"Exactly," said Eric. "I feel like I'm ready to tackle that talk now."

"Great," said Bill. "What do you think you want to say?"

"I'm not sure," said Eric. "I was hoping we could figure that out."

"Well, before you do that, I think you may be getting ahead of yourself."

"What do you mean?"

"For starters, have you ever had this kind of conversation with Hitomi? Do you even know if the two of you are on the same page about money?"

"I know we never argue about money, but we never really talk about it much, either."

"Well," said Bill, "I think that's where you need to start. I love the fact that you want to have the conversation with your kids, but it may be better to start with your wife first."

"OK," said Eric. "That make sense. But I'm not sure what we would talk about."

"Ask questions, said Bill. "That would be a great place for the two of you to start."

"What kind of questions?"

"I recommend you talk about ends rather than means."

"What do you mean?"

"Well, for many people, money is a means to an end. There

are certain goals people have in life, and money can help them achieved those goals. So, you need to start talking about what your goals are. What do the two of you want to achieve in life? How do you want to live? And since it looks like there's a good chance your money may outlive you, what are your goals for your wealth? Do you want to die on top of a big stack of gold bricks, or are there other things you want your wealth to achieve after you are long gone?"

"I'm realizing something," Eric said. "I spend most of my life thinking about means, but I don't invest much time or energy in thinking about ends."

"You're far from alone in that. But the question is, do you want to change it?"

"Two years ago, I wouldn't have cared much about all of this. But following our little near-death experience, I now realize this is way too important for me to ignore."

"Well, I'm truly sorry my plane scared the heck out of you, but I'm glad you decided to do something proactive."

"So where do I start?"

"Start a list of questions you would like to discuss with Hitomi. Once you have twenty or thirty good questions, take her out for a nice, long dinner and start asking. You probably won't have everything figured out by the time dessert arrives, but that's okay. The goal is to start talking about the things that matter to the two of you."

"Frankly, this sounds like one of the easiest and most interesting assignments you've given me!"

"Excellent," Bill said. "And by the way, compliments on your extra-credit work!"

AN INQUISITIVE FELLOW

A week later, Eric showed Bill his list of questions.

"It only has forty-seven questions so far," Eric said, "but I'm not done yet."

"My," said Bill. "Aren't you an inquisitive fellow!"

Eric read off some of the questions he thought could help start a good conversation with Hitomi.

What's your goal in life?

Do you think money is a good thing, a bad thing, or neutral?

What's your heart's desire for our daughters' lives, now and in the future?

After you die, what do you want your obituary in the San Jose Mercury News *to say?*

"Good questions," said Bill. "So how did the conversation go?"

"It was amazing. I learned things about Hitomi and how she grew up that I never knew before. And I talked to her about my father's philosophy on fat cats. We didn't settle many of the questions we discussed, but we learned a lot about each other's views on wealth and what's meaningful in life."

Bill beamed like a proud father.

"I'm so happy for you. So many people never take the time to discuss these deeper things in life. They spend their days focusing on means, but never take the time to discuss ends."

"You know, when we got down in the weeds on some of these issues, we realized there are some cases where we are on the same page, but other cases where we seem miles apart."

"For example?"

"Well, one example is philanthropy, or charitable giving, or whatever you call it. Hitomi believes in it and wants to do it. But I grew up skeptical of charities. My dad always said big charities were like big companies—all were run by fat cats."

"Sounds like these fat cats are multiplying! So where did you leave everything?"

"We made two main decisions. First, Hitomi came up with a brilliant idea for getting the girls involved in giving to charity. She calls it the Charity Challenge. She and I are going to give each of the girls $10,000 that they can give to a charity of their choice, but only after they have done some homework to research which charities are most effective and trustworthy."

"Nice."

"We're also going to revive our old tradition of date nights. We're going to try to go out to dinner once a week and spend at least some of our time talking about some of these deeper questions I've got written down."

"Keep me posted," said Bill, who was on his way to Borneo. "Catch me up in a couple of weeks."

"Will do," said Eric.

COLD TURKEY

"Borneo was awesome," said Bill. "How were things back here?"

"More billion-dollar IPOs. More billion-dollar mergers. Just a couple more average weeks in the Valley."

"I guess," said Bill.

"But the big news for us is closer to home. This Thanksgiving, the girls will be here, and Hitomi and I decided that's when we would have our first family conversation about money."

"Tell me more."

Eric said he and Hitomi were continuing to have good date-night conversations about "means and ends." Now, spontaneous conversations about money and values were popping up at other times of the week.

"We've been talking about what our core values are, and how we want that to frame how we talk to the girls about money. Like we said, it's all about means and ends, but we're still trying to clarify what some of our ends are."

"It's complicated stuff," Bill said, "but so important to discuss. Maybe more guys in the Valley should take a ride on some planes with bad carburetors!"

"I'm not sure about that. But thanks to you and our little adventure, we are going to start having some of the talks with our daughters that we should have had years ago."

"That sounds great, but before you credit me with this idea, let me ask you a question."

"Shoot."

"OK. Consider this: instead of having the all-important means and ends conversation with your kids at Thanksgiving, how about just starting the conversation then?"

"What do you mean?"

"Rather than trying to have this conversation cold turkey, so to speak, during your holiday celebration, why not start the conversation, and invite your girls to talk about it further later on? You and Hitomi have been talking about this for some time now, but your girls may not be up to speed.

"My suggestion is that you get the four of you together to briefly introduce the topic and invite them to start discussing it with you. They may need some time to think about some of the questions you and Hitomi have been weighing.

"If they want to dive into the topic right there in the middle of the Thanksgiving holiday, then you can dive into it, too. I just want to make sure you don't force the issue, or try to have a conversation that people aren't ready for."

"That makes sense," Eric said. "We will focus on hot turkey, not cold turkey!"

FAMILY MEETING 1.0

Eric and Hitomi honed their pitch. It only took four minutes and thirty-two seconds to explain their idea to Emma and Isabella and invite them to start joining them in discussions about family "means and ends."

Eric gave Bill a step-by-step summary of the family's first-ever official conversation about money:

I started by sharing what it was like to grow up with a father who was suspicious of corporate fat cats.

"That makes sense," said Isabella. "Some of my friends' dads talk about money all the time, but you never do. Now I see why."

Hitomi then talked to the girls about her belief in philanthropy.

"It was wealthy donors in Japan who founded the robotics contest I won there," she said, "and it was American donors who founded the scholarships that brought me to America.

Now it's my turn to give and help others."

Then Hitomi and I presented the girls with our Charity Challenge.

"One of the goals of charity is simply to give," Hitomi told them. "That's important. But an equally important goal is to impact the world for the better. Your father and I are giving the two of you $10,000 to give to a charity of your choice, but we want you to defend your choice with research showing the charity is effective at what it does and efficient in the use of donor funds."

We also gave each of the girls a copy of my "Means and Ends Questions." I honed the list down to the bare minimum, asking my girls a few basic but important questions about their lives, their values, their goals, and their passions.

Emma was excited to start the process, and was grateful that her mom and dad had provided some seed funding to get her charitable giving started.

"I'm glad we're going to start having this conversation," she said.

We all agreed we would start weaving some of these topics into our regular family conversations via phone and video. And we decided that the next time the four of us are together again, we would plan on having that deep-dive talk about family values and finances.

"Wow," said Bill. "It seemed like your first conversation was a huge hit."

"It really was," said Eric. "Plenty of hot turkey for all."

"SUCCESS" PART 1

In the coming months, Eric repeatedly did the same thing with his daughters that Bill had been doing with him. He asked Emma and Isabella probing questions and listened deeply to their answers.

In one of his questions, he asked them to define success.

"How do you define success in life? And in what ways would you say your definition is similar to or different from others you have heard?"

OK, technically that was actually two questions. But Eric wanted his girls to do two things: articulate their definitions of success, and compare and contrast their definition to those of others.

Eric found it interesting that neither one of his daughters defined success in terms of money. Both considered family very important in success. Both also said they wanted to impact the world for the better, but they had differing ideas about how to do that.

Eric also asked the girls about their research into the charity they would support. Emma gave him a brief report.

"Isabella and I have different priorities, so we decided to each use our $10,000 for two separate charities," she said, "one that Isabella chooses, and one that I choose."

"That makes sense," said Eric, "plus that means you get to research two organizations, not just one."

"Exactly," Isabella said.

"Let's talk about that in our next phone conversation."

CHARITY CHALLENGE PROGRESS REPORT

Eric and Hitomi scheduled a four-way phone chat with their two daughters to review their progress on the Charity Challenge.

Emma went first.

"I decided I wanted to do something to help America's military veterans," Emma said. "I hear a lot of people publicly go on and on about how they respect our veterans, but how many people actually help vets deal with all the challenges they face, from employment to post-traumatic stress injury to homelessness?"

"Do you think your friendships with children of military veterans impacted your decision?" Eric asked.

"Definitely," she said. "So on a heart level, I was really passionate about this. But then when I started doing some of the research, I found that some veteran charities, including one called the Wounded Warrior Project, raised millions of dollars, but then wasted much of it on overhead, high salaries, and fundraising rather than really helping veterans."

She talked about doing the two kinds of research Hitomi had suggested. She did Google searches to find news reports about charities' performance and practices. And she spent hours poring over ratings from charity watchdog organizations like Charity Navigator, which compiles data on thousands of charitable organizations.

"You would never know how much information is out there, both good and bad," she said. "And while the Wounded Warrior Project seems to have cleaned up its act in the last couple of years, in the end I decided to give all $10,000 to a small but highly rated charity that trains and provides service dogs to veterans dealing with injuries and post-traumatic stress."

"And how do you feel about that?" asked Eric.

"It feels great," she says. "I just keep picturing wounded, weary vets getting service dogs that can help them physically and emotionally."

Isabella decided to give her $10,000 to RefugeeAssist, the organization she worked for, so it could provide emergency food and water to displaced victims of the long-running Syrian war.

"It was interesting to conduct research on my own organization," she said. "I was surprised to see that we spend only seventy-five cents of every dollar on refugee program services, but I gave to a special program where every cent will be used to acquire and deliver food and water for Syrian refugees."

"Your generous gift may actually save people's lives," said Hitomi.

"Yes, I believe it will," set Isabella. "That makes me very happy deep down."

"Me too" said Hitomi.

"SUCCESS" PART 2

In another question, Eric asked his daughters to think about success beyond this life.

"Girls, one of these days your dear old dad is going to breathe his last breath. My obituary will mention my work with FinSoft, but I hope that's not all anyone remembers about me. What about you? If you were to die tomorrow, what would you want your obituaries to say? What would you want your legacy to be?"

Eric wasn't sure what kind of response he would get from asking his daughters questions about their legacies while they were still in the middle of trying to figure out their lives. But he wasn't looking for their answers to this question as much as he was trying to plant a seed.

He explained to Bill what he was trying to do when the two of them got together for breakfast.

"It seems like people are going to have a legacy one way or the other," Eric said. "It's either going to be intentional, based on what you plan, or it's going to be accidental, based on what happens in life. I want my girls to write their own legacy rather than having it written for them by other factors in their lives."

"That makes perfect sense," said Bill, "particularly coming from a man who saw his life flash before his eyes!"

"GETTING MY HOUSE IN ORDER"

Bill and Eric decided to celebrate the one-year anniversary of their Baja trip in style, meeting for steaks and beers at a local pub.

"So," Eric asked, "what's something significant you did with your life in the last year?"

"I replaced the carburetor in my airplane," said Bill, laughing. "That's significant to me. What about you?"

"I guess you could say I'm finally getting my house in order."

"That probably doesn't mean you are busy vacuuming and washing windows."

"No," said Eric. "It's all that unfinished business I thought about while the plane was going down and worried about during my sleepless nights.

"I realize I have been blessed. I kind of stumbled into success, but I don't want to stumble into my legacy. I want to be intentional about that. I want to do what I can to prepare Hitomi for life without me, should that happen. Meanwhile, I want to do what I can to prepare all of us for success in life, and beyond."

"Eric, you've been asking this question of your daughters lately, so let me ask you something. How do *you* define success in creating any kind of legacy you seek to create?"

"I'm not sure I can answer that. But I think Hitomi and I are pretty much on the same page now. We want our wealth to help our girls experience success, not to shelter them from the world.

"And as long as the company continues generating more income than we will ever be able to go through in even a dozen lifetimes, we want to leave a legacy for our family and beyond."

"I guess that's probably better than blowing it all on booze or gambling!" said Bill. "Let's talk more about what you want to do next time we meet."

THE RIGHT PERSON FOR THE JOB

Bill and Eric got together the next Friday morning to discuss Eric's plan to get his financial house in order.

"That's my goal," said Eric. "We've suddenly found ourselves generating the kind of wealth we never even dreamed about in my family, and I want all this to leave some kind of mark. I want to make sure we take care of Hitomi and the girls. That's the bottom line. But we also want to use some of our wealth to make the world a slightly better place."

"That's wonderful," said Bill. "Do you know what part of the world you want to impact, or how?"

"Not really," said Eric. "In fact, the more I think about all of this, the more confused I seem to get. I don't know much about managing investments. And there seems to be a zillion ways of setting up retirement accounts for the kids."

"At least a billion," said Bill.

"So, you've been around. What kind of professional help do I need to navigate these turbulent waters?"

"Well, most people seem to work with a variety of professionals. You can start with a certified public accountant to help you keep track of everything, and you will probably also need to talk to some insurance experts."

"I know a good CPA, but I'm in the dark about insurance. Do you know anybody?"

"Yeah, I could recommend a few people I like. You also need to figure out what roles the various family members will take."

"What do you mean?"

"Well, right now it sounds like you are the one person driving this for the whole family. But what happens if you aren't there anymore? Will Hitomi take over responsibility for overseeing the family assets? And what if you and she both die? Would either one of your girls be willing to act as executor of your will and other affairs?"

"Hmmm," said Eric. "I hadn't really thought about that."

"You can have a great plan, but it needs to be something that survives you."

"I'm not even sure I have a great plan," Eric said. "I only have some ideas, or rather some sentences scrawled in a file folder. I have some hopes for what I want to do, but I wouldn't call it a plan."

"In that case, I think you may need a guru."

"Do you mean some kind of Eastern religious guru?"

"No. A money guru. Someone who can help you translate your ideas into dollars and cents. Think of this person as your personal COO. Which reminds me, how's your corporate COO working out?"

"He's doing great. I can never thank you enough for leading me through that whole process. The company is better managed, and I have part of my life back."

"Well, I could introduce you to a couple of possible money gurus, too. Like with your COO, getting the right person for the job can make all the difference."

"Makes sense."

"I think the right person could help you and Hitomi get on the same page about your goals, and help you put your goals into a concrete plan that works for you, for her, for your girls, and even the parts of the world you want to impact. The right person could help you quit worrying and start doing what you want to do."

"Well, since this is coming from the man who saved my life with the right COO, I should probably give this a try, too. Let me talk to Hitomi and I'll get back to you."

"Great. See you next week."

"JUST DO IT"

Bill arrived early for their next meeting at Bill's Café, but Eric was running late, so Bill got out the little notebook and felt-tip pen he always carried around with him and jotted down five of the key points he and Eric had been discussing over the past year.

Wealth ≠ $

Relationships > $

Talk it over

Seek guidance

"Just Do It"

After Eric arrived, the two men ordered breakfast and caught up.

"So, do you have any news on the 'getting your house in order' front?" asked Bill. "How did your talk with Hitomi go?"

"It went well," said Eric. "She has always urged me to be more intentional about our affairs. She and I would both love to meet your money guru."

"That's good news," Bill said. "I can set up a meeting for you."

"Great!"

As the two talked, Bill reviewed the notes he had jotted down on his notebook page.

"These are my notes on some of the key things we've been discussing. Let's do a quick review."

Eric looked at the notes on the page, but could make little sense out of the dozen or so words and symbols.

"You are a master of understatement!" said Eric. "So, what does all this mean?"

"OK, let me unpack it all. Do you remember a couple of months ago we talked about how wealth is more than money and financial assets"

"That's point number one. Money does not equal wealth. Money can be a part of a person's wealth, but it's not the whole enchilada, as some people think."

"Yeah," said Eric. "We talked about how a person's health could be part of their wealth, or even their family name and reputation."

"Exactly," said Bill. "The next squiggles say that our relationships are some of the most valuable things we have."

"I hadn't thought about that very much before, but thanks to you pestering me, I know that's true."

"The next one's simple," said Bill. "People need to talk about money, how they feel about it, what they want to do with it."

"Amen," said Eric. "Money is something our family never really talked about before now. It's funny. I was so worried that family talks about money wouldn't go anywhere. But they've been some of the best talk we've had in years."

"You're fortunate!" said Bill. "And the next two points are pretty straightforward. Seek guidance from somebody who knows all about assets and can help you convert your ideas into a real plan."

"Check," said Eric.

"And I stole Nike's slogan for this last one, but the point was simple. To put it frankly, you should start working on this sooner rather than later."

"It can't be soon enough for me," said Eric. "I'm ready to start working this out right now."

Bill gave Eric a curious look.

"What?" asked Eric.

"I just had an idea."

"What is it?"

"After our breakfast I have a meeting set up with Veronica, my wealth advisor. I could introduce you if you would like to tag along. Would you like to meet her?"

"Let's do it!" said Eric.

PART 4:

A PLAN THAT WORKS

NICE, WITH NO ICE

Bill and Eric rode the elevator up to the wealth advisory office where Veronica was a vice president. A video screen just inside the office doors read, "Welcome, Bill!"

"Well, hello Bill," said Julie, the front office manager and receptionist. "How was Borneo?"

"Hi, Julie," said Bill. "It was totally awesome, thank you! And this is my good friend, Eric."

"Any friend of Bill's is a friend of ours," said Julie, as she shook Eric's hand. "Veronica is wrapping up a call, but the two of you can cool your heels for a minute in our conference room."

Entering the room, which offered an expansive view of the Valley, Bill headed for a chair near the drinks and snacks.

"Julie, you remembered," said Bill, biting into a freshly cooked chocolate chip cookie, his favorite kind, and washing it down with a Diet Coke with no ice, as he preferred.

"What can I get you, Eric?"

"Water will be fine, thanks."

Bill was still chewing his first cookie when Dave, the company's founder and CEO, popped his head into the conference room and said hello.

"Having better luck with that new carburetor than you were with the old one?" Dave joked.

"Much better," said Bill. "And Dave, I want you to meet my good friend, Eric. He runs one of the Valley's fastest-growing companies."

"Congratulations, Eric," said Dave. "Nice to meet you."

"These people seem downright friendly!" Eric said. "Not pushy, just friendly."

"That's why I've worked with them for twenty years," said Bill. "The nice you see is more than skin-deep."

Dave had just left the conference room when a smiling Veronica entered. Bill stood and gave her a hug before she reached out her hand to greet Eric.

"This is my good friend, Eric," he said. "He runs a company in the Valley, and he came along to see if he could set up his own meeting with you."

"Great," said Veronica. "So, Eric, what's on your mind?"

"My wife and I have been talking, and we need someone to help us translate some of our ideas into a real plan."

"Eric, that sounds like something we can do," she said. "Julie will be glad to set up something that works for you and your wife. What's her name?"

"Hitomi," said Eric. "And by the way, the two of us want a plan not only for ourselves, but also for our daughters. And we also want to impact the world through some philanthropic giving, but we don't have a clue about how to do that."

"You came to the right place," said Veronica. "Philanthropy is one of our core passions, and we've been helping Valley donors for decades. I will look forward to helping the two of you come up with a plan that works for you."

"That would be wonderful," said Eric. "Thank you."

EPILOGUE

A WHALE OF A TIME

Months later, Bill and Eric paid a return visit to Baja to watch the whales, eat relaxed meals, drink too many beers, and talk about whatever came to their minds.

It had been another year of rapid growth for FinSoft, which meant it had been a busy year for Eric. But overall, work was easier now that his COO, who was well into his second year running the company, was protecting Eric from stress and burnout.

It had also been a great year for Eric's family, having the regular kinds of talks about life and money that they had avoided for so many years.

The time flew as the two men—now closer friends and trusted allies—rested and relaxed. Before long it was time to pack up for the flight back home in Bill's plane.

But before they boarded, Eric asked Bill to sit down.

"I've got something for you," he said, handing Bill a small wrapped gift. "It's not much, really, just a symbol of our friendship."

Bill unwrapped the paper to find a plaque. Attached to the plaque was a used carburetor. Underneath the carburetor were the words:

"To Bill: My life-saving (but potentially lethal) friend. With my love and affection, Eric."

Bill's face lit up as he read the plaque.

"What a nice sentiment, wonderfully delivered!" said Bill.

"It's from the heart," Eric said.

"I can tell, Eric. Thank you."

Their packing finished, the two men clambered into Bill's plane, but Eric had one more thing to say before Bill started up the engine.

"Bill, I just want you to know that no matter what happens to us on the way home, I feel ready for it now."

"Well, hopefully I won't require you to act on that!"

"Agreed," said Eric. "But it's a good feeling not to worry."

"Yes," said Bill. "It's the best."

ABOUT THE AUTHOR

Frank Reilly is President of Reilly Financial Advisors, a firm he founded with his father. He has since worked with generations of clients to help them secure their financial legacies and provide for their heirs. His passion for doing so is driven from his desire to help others realize and successfully navigate their financial purpose. Equally as important, Frank has the desire to maintain the family culture of the business he and his father started, continuing that legacy to help future generations.

Before starting with the company, Frank worked with a leading technology, brokerage, and investment advisor platform for financial advisors.

Frank holds a Bachelor of Science and a Master's Degree in International Business from the United States International University and has earned the FINRA Series 4, 7, 24, 63, and 65 licenses.

In his free time, he enjoys traveling with his wife, Gina, and their five children, as well as teaching middle school, high school and college-level courses in finance, investing and economics, skiing, and wine tasting.

Reilly Financial Advisors

CREATE A PLAN THAT WORKS

Knowing how to navigate through the different stages of life can help set you and your family up for success for generations to come.

Reilly Financial Advisors is a fee-only Registered Investment Advisor established in 1999 to provide clients with an integrated approach to all their financial needs. By acting in Fiduciary Standard, we are responsible for putting clients' best interests first, before that of our own compensation.

Our core purpose as a firm is to help our clients define and achieve their individual financial goals through truthfulness, honesty, reliability, and caring.

WE ARE EAGER TO HELP YOU.

Call 800-682-3237 or email us at

info@rfawealth.com | www.rfawealth.com